Wandering Woman: North Dakota

The Ultimate Road Trip: One Woman's Journey Across the United States by RV

Julie Bettendorf

Contents

Introduction

"Not all who wander are lost." JRR Tolkien

Are you sure? I thought to myself, as I tried not to panic. I was a long way from anything familiar, but that was how it should be. I had driven thousands of miles on dusty, pothole-filled roads. It's often on the worst roads that you can discover something truly amazing.

My dusty CRV was parked beside me, containing one restless dog and a variety of snack bags, all empty by now. There were no buildings in sight, no cars or people or movement at all. Only the constant humming of the insects as they buzzed around my head.

I turned to my left – another straight road that trailed off into the distance. I glanced over to the right, then behind me – two more barely discernible roads stretched out into the abyss. I was in a four-way intersection with no signs, no sense of direction, and no sign of life for several miles. No cell service either. *Damn*, I thought. *I'm lost.*

How did I get here? I couldn't help but feel like this little intersection was a cruel metaphor for life. I began to daydream, imagining each road might transport me back to a different time, a different role in my life, and a different me.

If I took the road from whence I came, it could lead me all the way back to Oregon, back to my cheating third husband, back to a life of loneliness and solitude. There is no greater loneliness than being married to someone who isn't actually present in your life.

If I took the road to my left, perhaps it could take me back to my career as a dental hygienist, a job I hated deep down in my soul. There is something so disengaging about cleaning teeth for a living. It's a disgusting, smelly way to get a paycheck. It pays well, which is great, but the best part is the huge gob of friends I enjoy to this day.

Or maybe the road to my right, *yes – maybe that's the path*, I imagined. Maybe it could take me back to my real treasure, my kids. Back to their smiling, innocent faces as toddlers, as they danced around the Christmas tree and their father and I were still married. Back when they still needed me for every little thing.

But, that was just it. I didn't feel needed anymore. My kids weren't toddlers anymore – they were both full-grown adults, and far too busy for me. My dental buddies were still working, but I wasn't. Dental hygiene had robbed me of the cartilage in my fingers, giving me severe, disabling arthritis. And, I wouldn't be returning to any more husbands either, because three marriages were quite enough for me.

All three of these paths, all three of these roles – the wife, the mother, and the dental hygienist – had seemingly been stripped from me within a year. I was lost and looking to find myself again.

The funny thing about this phrase, "not all who wander are lost" – is that, in my experience, wandering and being lost walk hand-in-hand with one another, and the expression can be flipped. In my experience, not all who are lost are wandering, and that is a real disservice to the beauty and clarity that the world has to offer.

When one becomes lost, wandering is the only option to guide oneself back to a path. After all, one could not come upon any dirt path at all without wandering.

I began wandering at an early age, both with my mind and with my feet. At eight years old, I was reading a book about archaeology and dreaming of one day seeing Egypt. I didn't follow a traditional path in high school either, going heavily into foreign languages, in hopes of one day using them.

At twenty-five years old, I divorced my first husband (the dental student who talked me into becoming a dental hygienist so I could work for him) and decided to give traveling a real shot. I took off for the Andes and Macchu Picchu, climbing up ancient Inca stone steps to reach the magnificent ruins.

Anyone who has been to Macchu Picchu will tell you there is something ethereal and deeply spiritual about the place. The ruins stretch out across the emerald green mountains, way up in the middle of the sky. Macchu Picchu gave me my first experience of feeling history. This trip inspired me to come back and complete a degree in archaeology, and I've been wandering ever since.

More travel followed including a backpack trip around Europe for three months, by myself, and trips to Britain, Italy, and Greece. I visited the burial places of Crusaders, mummies, and ancient kings. I happened upon the castle of my namesake in Bettendorf, Luxembourg, and wandered my way through European history.

My favorite excursion by far was finally seeing Egypt with my daughter in 2012. Just like my childhood dream envisioned, I rode a camel beneath the pyramids of Giza, with my head wrapped in some man's sweaty turban. It was perfect.

Traveling has always been my own personal antidote to pain. I went to Mexico after my first and second divorces, Canada after my third, and Italy after my dad died. Call it avoidance if you want, but I call it an accelerated form of healing in the purest sense of the word. I believe travel can heal your soul.

Wandering has always worked its wonders on me – made me feel renewed, rejoiceful, grateful, and purposeful. It's been my medicine.

So, as I stood in that intersection, I once again wondered how wandering had led me so astray this time. *What the hell am I supposed to do now?* It was then that I realized that one last path had not been considered yet – the path which stretched straight out in front of me. *Which role does this represent?* I pondered.

The answer smacked me in the face.

That last dirt road – the only path that could take me where I wanted to go, the only path that ever truly healed me or showed me the way – was the path of the traveler. The wife, the mother, and the hygienist roles – though valued in their time – were sitting in the bleachers now. It was time to welcome and enable my boldest, bravest, and perhaps most pivotal role yet:

The role of the Wandering Woman.

Welcome to Wandering Woman

This book is for you – the grieving empty nester mom, the begrudged housewife, the woman in need of a drastic change in her life. Really, this book is for anyone with a passion for traveling. If you feel lost with no sense of direction or purpose in life, that's a bonus – this book will be even more appealing to you. And lastly, if you're a man reading this book, congratulations for holding a book with the word woman in the title. You're contributing to gender equality, and that's pretty neat.

I decided to combine three of my dearest loves – travel, history, and archaeology – and put them into a book because I believe wandering has the power to change your life. I have been to many areas of the world and have enjoyed too many outstanding experiences to list. However, by the time both my children moved out in 2017, I realized I was a stranger in my own country. It was the perfect time to explore a new country (my own) and discover a new me at the same time. I have been traveling for five years now, and I've upgraded to a small RV. I also have a new traveling companion, another sweet Sheltie, named Rosie. **Wandering Woman** is the chronicle of my journey across the United States, discovering the joy of getting lost and finding myself along the way.

Why You Need to Take a Road Trip

A *merica, the beautiful?* I sure think so, but I didn't realize just how beautiful our country is until I embarked on traveling across the United States, full time, in a small RV.

The United States offers something for everyone. From spectacular beaches, austere mountains, to rolling plains, our country has it all. It's difficult to comprehend just how large and impressive our scenery is, until you experience it first-hand, with the ultimate road trip.

I also realized just how much of our history is missing from U.S. history I was taught as a kid. The history of our country didn't begin with the pilgrims landing on Plymouth Rock in the 1600s. Our history is far more ancient, with rock art and archaeological sites dating back over 12,000 years.

We owe a tremendous debt to early pioneers who tamed our land. The Mormons and other groups ventured into the great unknown with their families and their worldly possessions. Some of them pulled cumbersome handcarts across the country to settle in inhospitable, dangerous locations.

The goal of **Wandering Woman** is to bring history back to life and make it interesting again. I am presenting some famous sites, and many little-known ones. You will take the road-less-traveled with me, while we explore ghost towns, rock art sites, archaeological sites, and museums, to discover the colorful tapestry that is our country.

I present some history, including dates, but my goal is to present more of the real-life stories of history, including ghost stories, profiles in history, voices from the past, and moments in time, to give you, the reader, a deeper understanding of the context of history.

This is by no means an exhaustive list of places to visit. In fact, I encourage you to discover America for yourself, as I am doing, by making a trek across the land by car or RV. You can venture forth as the early explorers did, just a little more comfortably, with a lot less hardship.

I hope you enjoy this book and take a little time out to discover our beautiful country, and maybe even discover yourself in the process.

Safe Travels,

Julie Bettendorf

Welcome to North Dakota

The Peace Garden State

N orth Dakota has a spiritual quality about it, from vast, rolling prairies, to sparkling lakes. There is a lot of history in North Dakota too, from pioneer sites to military forts. North Dakota has something for everyone.

5 Things to Love About North Dakota:

- The scenic beauty of the mighty Missouri River

- Ancient inscriptions at Writing Rock State Historical Site

- Lewis & Clark history at sites like Fort Mandan

- Early fur trading history from Fort Union Trading Post

- Old military forts like Fort Totten

Dreams of North Dakota

"When my parents first arrived there, North Dakota had just been admitted to the Union, and the country was still wild and harsh." **Lawrence Welk**

"My grandmother raised five children during the Depression by herself. At 50, she threw her sewing machine into the back of a pickup truck and drove from North Dakota to California. She was a real survivor, so that's my stock. That's how I want my kids to be too." **Michelle Pfeiffer**

"'I was born in a very small town in North Dakota, a town of only about 350 people. I lived there until I was 13. It was a marvelous advantage to grow up in a small town where you knew everybody." **Warren Christopher**

Famous Citizens of North Dakota

Warren Christopher (1925–2011) U.S. Secretary of State 1993–97

Angie Dickinson (born 1931) Emmy and Golden Globe award-winning actress

Louis L'Amour (1908–1988) western author

Peggy Lee (1920–2002) three-time Grammy award-winning singer-songwriter

Sacajawea (1788–1812) guide on the Lewis and Clark Expedition

Eric Sevareid (1912–1992) TV journalist

Lawrence Welk (1903–1992) bandleader, entertainer, TV personality

Early North Dakota

Fort Abercrombie Brewery 1868

Early North Dakota Elections

Early North Dakota Citizens

Writing Rock
State Historic Site

T he **_Writing Rock State Historic Site_** contains two myste-
rious boulders covered with petroglyphs. The petroglyphs
are striking, especially the thunderbird effigies. One boulder is
four and one-half feet high and four feet wide. The smaller boulder is three and one-half feet long, two feet wide, and one and
one-half feet high.

Thunderbirds have been a sacred design among the Native Americans for at least 2000 years and are believed to bring about thun-
der and lightning storms. A thunderbird's eyes were believed to
shoot out lightning, and their wings created the wind. The Writing
Rock Petroglyphs are believed to be at least 300 to 1000 years old.

They are now housed in a fenced stone shelter to protect them from the environment and vandalism.

How to get to Writing Rock State Historic Site:

The Writing Rock State Historic Site is located 14.5 miles north-east of Grenora.

A word about petroglyphs and pictographs:

Petroglyphs were made by taking river rock and heating it, and then cooling it suddenly so it cracks to form a sharp tool. This tool was used to chisel along with another stone for a hammer to peck or incise the designs on rock. A thick coating called a patina was removed to expose the lighter rock underneath.

Pictographs, are painted instead of incised. They are drawn pictures using minerals like hematite mixed with a binder such as animal fat, urine, or oil to make paint.

Fort Buford State Historic Site

*F**ort Buford** was built in 1866, and named after Major John Buford, a Union commander during the Battle of Gettysburg. The fort functioned to protect the area of the Missouri and Yellowstone rivers, and provide supplies for soldiers headed west.

The fort is a place of great historical significance. It was here that Sitting Bull surrendered to Commander David Brotherton in 1881, which ended the Plains Indian wars.

The large building is a reconstruction of the infantry barracks. The first barracks was built in 1867 out of adobe. The adobe structure was remodeled in 1873 to include siding and wood windows.

This stone building is the powder magazine, where ammunition was stored. The structure is built of sandstone from a quarry nearby.

One of the more sobering places in Fort Buford is the cemetery. There are 161 restored headstones, but only 8 people are buried there. The rest have been removed, most to the Battle of the Little Bighorn Cemetery. The Fort Buford Cemetery is a fascinating place where soldiers, Native Americans, and ordinary citizens were all buried together.

The telegraph was completed in 1878, enabling communication to other forts and areas of the frontier. Soldiers of the fort helped to construct the telegraph lines. Fort Buford was abandoned in 1895.

How to get to Fort Buford State Historic Site:

Fort Buford is located at 15349 39th Ln NW, in Williston.

Profiles in history:

Sitting Bull, also known as Tatanka-iyotanka, was born in 1831 in what is now South Dakota. He became a chief of a tribe when he was in his late twenties. Sitting Bull was a spiritual and political leader who united the tribes to act against the expansion of settlers. After defeating Custer, Sitting Bull and his people went up into Canada, returning to the US in 1881 to surrender. He was killed December 15, 1890 by Indian police on the Standing Rock Reservation in South Dakota. Donovan

Voices from the past:

"I surrender this rifle to you through my young son, who I now desire to teach in this manner, now that he has become a friend of the American people. I wish to teach him the habits of the whites and to have him educated as their sons are educated. I wish it to be remembered that I was the last man in my tribe to surrender my rifle..." **Sitting Bull, as recorded by Joe Culbertson, Indian Scout**

Fort Union Trading Post

*F*ort *Union* was a critical trading post, active from 1828 to 1867. The fort promoted trade between tribes of the Northern Plains, trappers, and explorers from many countries. Fort Union lasted the longest of any trading post.

The present fort has been reconstructed on the foundations of the original fort. It's a fascinating place, and as you enter, you will see the massive robe press out front, which would press and package ten buffalo robes to be shipped at a later date.

The walls of the fort are 18 feet high. The painting above the south gate commemorates an 1831 treaty between the Assiniboine and Blackfeet tribes, which was facilitated by the manager of the fort.

Areas to visit include the storeroom, the smokehouse, and soldier's quarters. The defensive towers, called bastions, are amazing structures, with cannons to defend the fort.

The first steamboat, the Yellowstone, reached Fort Union in 1832. Over time, the course of the Missouri River moved away from the bank, reducing river trade and travel to the trading post by water.

The fort also had several famous visitors in its lifetime including John James Audubon in 1843, Prince Maximillian of Wied in 1833, and artist George Catlin in 1832.

How to get to Fort Union Trading Post:

*F*ort Union Trading Post is located at 15550 Hwy 1804, in Williston.

Voices from the past:

"Our officers Gave...each head chief a meddel & a flag...a Suit of Cloaths and a quantity of Small Goods for their nations, cocked hats & feathers. Gave also a Steel corn mill to the Manden nation which please them verry much. " **Sergeant John Ordway, October 29, 1804**

"From the top of the hills we saw a grand panorama of a most extensive wilderness, with Fort Union beneath us and far away, as well as the Yellowstone River, and the lake across the river. The hills across the Missouri appeared quite low, and we could see the high prairie beyond, forming the background." **John James Audubon 1843**

Killdeer Mountain
Battlefield

K_illdeer Mountain Battlefield_ is located on land known by the Nakota as Tachawakute, or "the place where they kill deer."

On July 28, 1864, troops led by General Alfred Sully, attacked groups of Nakota, Dakota, and Lakota Sioux, led by Sitting Bull and Medicine Bear.

Sully's men fired cannon upon the Indians, many of whom desired peace with the whites. Estimates are that between 100 and 150 Sioux died. 5 soldiers lost their lives in the battle.

How to get to Killdeer Mountain Battlefield:

The Killdeer Mountain Battlefield is located on the Killdeer Mt. Battlefield Rd, near the town of Killdeer.

Fort Dilts

*F*ort Dilts has no structures. The site is dedicated to the memory of soldiers and pioneers who circled their wagons to protect themselves from an Indian attack in September, 1864.

Soldiers from the accompanying army, led by Captain James Fisk, stacked sod to create breastworks for defense.

The fort was named Fort Dilts to honor Corporal Jefferson Dilts, who died and was buried in the defensive walls. A total of nine people from the wagon train died, along with eight soldiers. The Sioux lost about two dozen warriors, and one of the wounded warriors was Sitting Bull.

Today, the site is a peaceful, serene expanse of wind-blown prairie. You can see the sod fortifications, graves, and wagon ruts.

How to get to Fort Dilts:

Fort Dilts is located on Fort Dilts Rd, near Rhame.

Profiles in history:

Corporal Jefferson Dilts was born in Ohio in 1832. Jefferson married Sarah Scott in 1847, and the couple had at least two sons. He became a soldier and a scout in the US Army. Dilts was part of a cavalry unit attached to a wagon train traveling to the gold fields in Montana.

The wagon train was attacked by Sioux warriors. Dilts rode back to the battlefield with several volunteers to protect the rear wagons. The volunteers would not engage the Sioux, so Dilts went on alone, engaging in hand to hand combat. After the battle, Dilts rode back to the wagon train, with two arrows in his chest, one in his back, and a knife wound to his neck.

Dilts died of his wounds one day before the wagon train was rescued. He is buried under the wall of the fort on the northwestern side. and memorialized by a tombstone at the historic site.

Douglas

T he small town of ***Douglas*** has historical significance for the Bettendorf family because my dad and many of his brothers and sisters grew up there. It's a great little prairie town.

My dad told me many stories about going to a one-room school-house out on the open prairie, so I decided to try and find the schoolhouse. He spoke of riding in a horse-drawn "bus" heated by a woodstove in the winter.

Douglas was full of helpful people, who aided me in my quest to find the school. With the help of the lovely people of Douglas, I found the schoolhouse, sitting by itself, on a hill out in the middle of the windswept prairie. I braved a barbed wire fence to get in and take photos of the school.

It's called the Crystal School. I was filled with emotion walking through this place, imagining my dad, aunts and uncles as little kids running around. I imagined my family looking out over the prairie through these windows.

How to get to Douglas:

Douglas is located off Hwy. 83 about 35 miles south of Minot.

A word about how history is lost:

History can be lost very easily and quickly, unless it is preserved in books or in memories. The Crystal School is a perfect example. I looked up a survey on the Crystal School which was completed in 2012. I read that the Crystal School was built in 1900, and it closed in 1959. There is a section on the survey which reads *"Feature Preservation Recommendation."* Unfortunately, the recommendation was *"no nomination potential."* It seems the Crystal School is just going to slowly decay out there on the prairie. I know there are often not enough funds to preserve our history, so we must all venture out and see our history before it is lost to time.

Voices from the past:

"...in the northwest corner of the frosted window, there was a clear spot and by standing on my tiptoes, I could peer out into the darkness and then I saw it. A dim, small light bobbing off in the distance. I let everyone know the bus was coming. Mom was busy making the lunches. Homemade bread with peanut butter and jelly or honey sandwiches. A cookie or bar packed in a small bucket with a handle on it. When you ordered jelly or honey from the mail order catalog it came in these handy one or two quart pails. We didn't have regular lunch boxes, like you would buy in town. I'd

heard some of the neighbors had to have lard on their bread. I thought a story like that may have been told to make the peanut butter and jelly taste better...

That particular morning it was 20 degrees below zero...I will never forget the crunching sound the horse's hoofs made on the hard, cold snow. I never minded the ride on the bus...it was one of the adventures of going to a country school...

My first eight years of school were spent at that two-room school-house in Rosemont Township, McLean County, North Dakota. Those years will never be forgotten. It's now the year 2004. Crystal School, as it was called, with the teacher's quarters between the lower and upper class rooms, still stands alone on the 10 acres of prairie, on top of a hill...It's quiet now, the horse barn and two privies are gone. The doors are closed, paint has all peeled off and the windows boarded up. On the steps sits a white cat. Is he waiting for the buses to bring the kids to school or hearing the peel of the bell, calling them in from recess?" **One Cold Winter Morning, by Bea (Bettendorf) Sorensen, March 2004.**

Knife River Indian Villages

Knife River Indian Villages has a long history. The Paleo-Indi-ans roamed the Knife River region from 11,000 to 6,000 BC. These were followed by Archaic peoples from 6,000 BC to 1 AD. The Woodland culture began farming the area in 1000 BC to 1000 AD.

When the Europeans arrived, the Mandan and Hidatsa had already lived in the area for 500 years. The two main sites in the Knife River complex are the Lower Hidatsa site, established around 1525 AD, and the Big Hidatsa site, established around 1600 AD.

The first European to enter the villages was the French-Canadian trader Verendrye in 1738, followed by David Thompson in 1797. These were followed by Lewis & Clark in 1804.

The smallpox epidemic of 1837 reduced their numbers, and the Mandan and Hidatsa were later joined by the Arikara from the south in 1862. In 1885, the tribes were forced to relocate to Fort Berthold Reservation.

The site also contains a fine museum full of interesting artifacts. One of my favorites is a water carrier made from a bison bladder.

How to get to Knife River Indian Villages:

The Knife River Indian Villages site is located 60 miles north of Bismarck, near the city of Stanton.

Fort Clark

N ot much remains of ***Fort Clark***, other than its history. Fort Clark was built by the Columbia Fur Company and named after William Clark, of the Lewis & Clark Expedition. Fur traders began trading with the neighboring tribes.

The Mandan built a village close to the fort in 1822. In 1837, a steamboat named the St. Peters docked at the fort. Passengers on the boat carried smallpox and infected the Mandan. 90 percent of the Mandan died.

The Arikara, a neighboring tribe, survived the epidemic and moved into the Mandan village. A Cholera epidemic in 1851 and a return of smallpox in 1856 reduced their numbers. The village was abandoned in 1862.

Today, as you walk around Fort Clark, you can see surface depressions which used to be houses, graves, storage pits, and other features.

How to get to Fort Clark Historic Site:

Fort Clark is located between the towns of Washburn and Stanton.

Fort Mandan

F*ort Mandan* is the site of the winter quarters of the Lewis
and Clark Expedition. When Lewis and Clark reached the

area, it was the site of the five towns of the Mandan and Hidatsa tribes, with a population close to that of Washington D.C. in 1804.

The exact location of Fort Mandan is unknown, but there is a wonderful reconstruction of the fort and a visitors center. The original Fort Mandan was built by members of Lewis and Clark's Corps of Discovery in 1804. They spent the winter of 1804 to 1805 there. They named the fort "Mandan in honour of our Neighbors."

French trader Touissant Charbonneau and his wife, Sacajawea, lived with the Hidatsa. Both were hired on as interpreters for the expedition. At Fort Mandan, Sacajawea gave birth to a boy, Jean Baptiste, which Clark nicknamed "Pomp."

The expedition left Fort Mandan in April 1805, after wintering there for five months. When they returned in 1806, most of the fort was washed away by the river.

How to get to Fort Mandan:

Fort Mandan is located at 838 28th Ave SW, in Washburn.

Profiles in history:

William Clark was born August 1, 1770, in Virginia. He was a friendly, extroverted person. After the Lewis and Clark Expedition, Clark became superintendent of Indian affairs in the Louisiana Territory, becoming Governor of Missouri territory in 1810. He died in St. Louis on Sept. 1, 1838, at the age of 68. [Peck]

Meriwether Lewis was born August 18, 1774. Lewis was a well-educated aristocrat. He became part of the Chosen Rifle Company where he met William Clark. Lewis was expedition leader and asked Clark to join him on the venture. Lewis died in October 1809, suddenly and violently at an inn where he was staying. There is controversy over whether he was murdered or committed suicide. He suffered from depression and consumed alcohol and opium. He was 35. [Peck]

York was born in 1770 and was William Clark's African American slave. He was responsible for carrying provisions, hunting game, gathering water and performing other tasks for Clark. York was occasionally ordered to dance, which "amused the crowd very much." York was sometimes paraded in front of Native Americans, who marveled at his muscular body and called him "big medicine." After the expedition, York requested to be freed, but Clark refused. He remained a slave until at least 1816, and died of cholera in 1832. Strahn

Sacajawea, also spelled Sakakawea, was born in Idaho around 1788, and was a member of the Lemhi Shoshone tribe. She was captured by Hidatsa when she was 12, and one year later, she was sold into marriage with Toussaint Charbonneau, a French-Canadian trapper. They lived among the Mandan in North Dakota. Sacajawea was pregnant and only 16 years old when she joined the Lewis and Clark Expedition as a guide and interpreter. Sacajawea was responsible for saving the journals of Lewis and Clark, when the records fell into the river. According to Native American oral traditions, Sacajawea died in 1884 and is buried in Wyoming. Other accounts list her death in 1812.

Seaman, the wonderful Newfoundland dog of the Lewis and Clark Expedition is immortalized with a statue. No one knows what happened to Seaman but an entry was found in an old book. The author, Timothy Alden, saw a dog collar in a museum in Alexandria, Virginia. The collar was inscribed with the words ***"The greatest traveller of my species. My name is SEAMAN, the dog of captain Meriwether Lewis, whom I accompanied to the Pacific ocean through the interior of the continent of North America."*** Alden stated that the dog returned with the expedition, and when Lewis died in 1809, Seaman grieved at the gravesite of his master and eventually died there.

Voices from the past:

"My dog would take the squirel in the water kill them and swimming bring them in his mouth to the boat." **Journal of Meriwether Lewis, September 11, 1804**

"One of the party wounded a beaver, and my dog as usual swam in to catch it, the beaver bit him through the hind leg and cut the artery; it was with great difficulty that I could stop the blood. I fear it will yet prove fatal to him." **Journal of Meriwether Lewis, May 19, 1805**

Lewis &
Clark Interpretive
Center

The ***Lewis & Clark Interpretive Center*** is close to Fort Mandan and contains some wonderful artifacts from the expedition.

Among the many artifacts are an amputation knife, medical saw, medical chest containing medicines from the 1800s, tins for medicines, and medicine bottles.

My favorite artifact is a button from William Clark's jacket. You can also see a hinge from Meriwether Lewis's journal, guns, and a sewing kit.

Another amazing artifact is one of the nearly 90 peace medals Lewis and Clark brought with them. Peace medals were given to Native American chiefs to promote peace, communication, and cooperation.

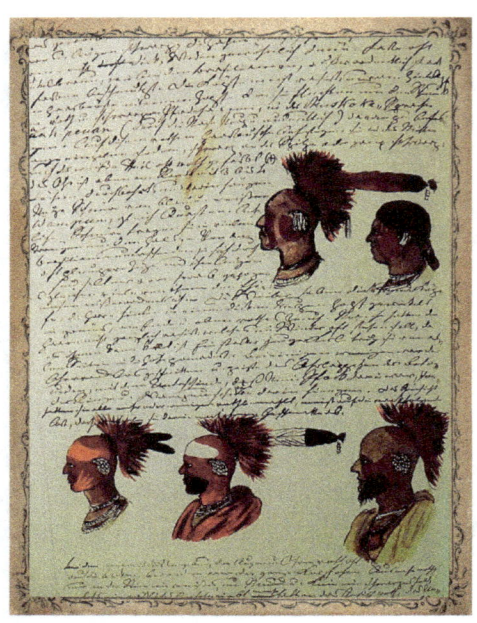

Don't miss the spectacular art works of Karl Bodmer, who accompanied the expedition. He was contracted by Prince Maximillian of Wied, who also accompanied the expedition.

How to get to the Lewis & Clark Interpretive Center:

The Lewis & Clark Interpretive Center is located at 2576 8th Street Southwest, in Washburn.

A word about the Lewis & Clark Expedition:

In 1803, President Thomas Jefferson funded the expedition with $2500. The group was to find the most direct water route to the Pacific. Meriwether Lewis, who was a family friend of Jefferson, was put in charge of the expedition. He enlisted his friend from the Indian campaigns, William Clark. Meriwether Lewis and his men left Pittsburgh on August 31, 1803. They stopped in Clarksville, Indiana, to pick up William Clark and additional men. The group left St. Louis, Missouri on May 15, 1804. When they left, Clark was 33, and Lewis was 29.

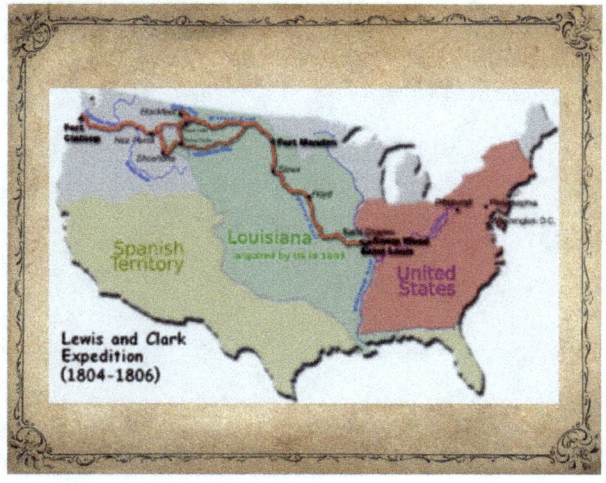

They spent their first winter among the Mandan tribe in North Dakota, establishing Fort Mandan. It was here that they added French explorer Charbonneau and his wife Sacajawea. They left Fort Mandan in April of 1805, heading up the Missouri River. They reached the Pacific Ocean in November of 1805. The journey would eventually take 28 months and the group would travel 8000 miles. [Jones]

Interesting facts about the Lewis & Clark Expedition:

Clark paid his interpreter Charbonneau a total of $500 and 33 and 1/3 cents for his services on the expedition.

There is a myth among the Nez Perce that the sister of Chief Red Grizzly Bear had a son with Clark. The boy had light hair and often proclaimed "Me Clark."

Venereal disease was common among the Indians they met. A few of the party suffered the effects from encounters with the women.

Gonorrhea was a frequent problem, and what Lewis called Louis Venerae.

Sacajawea was promised to another Indian man, but because she had a child with Charbonneau, the Indian didn't want her. During the expedition, Charbonneau hit Sacajawea and was reprimanded by Clark.

Early in the expedition, several men were court-martialed and whipped for "having uttered repeated expressions of a highly criminal and mutinous nature," and desertion.

Clark suffered from foot problems, and Lewis suffered from depression.

During the expedition, the group endured hunger, disease, subzero temperatures, blizzards, fierce rapids, grizzly bear attacks, thick clouds of mosquitoes, and repeated robberies by Indians. They also were reduced to eating their dogs and colts to stay alive.

They wrote nearly one million published words in journals of their trip.

Only 1 out of 9 practicing doctors actually had a medical degree in Lewis & Clark's time. Most were trained on-the-job, including Lewis and Clark.

Medications they took along including a variety of potent laxatives known as "thunderclappers."

They also brought along penile syringes to treat venereal disease by injecting a solution into the urethra.

Lancets were purchased for "therapeutic" bloodletting. Opium and a 10% opium solution known as Laudanum were used quite frequently on the trip.

An ointment made of ground beetles was used to create blisters, believed to act as a "counterirritant."

Lead acetate was used in "eyewashes" which were traded with Columbia Basin Indians.

Lewis & Clark campsites could be identified by archaeologists because of the mercury residue in the latrines, from medications the expeditions members were taking.

The total cost of all medical supplies was $90.60. Peck

Bismarck

B*ismarck* has a wonderful museum known as the ***North Dakota Heritage Center & State Museum***. Within the museum are several galleries containing everything from dinosaurs to the state archives, where I discovered some history about my dad's family.

The museum also contains Dakota, the 67 million year old dinosaur mummy. Dakota is a duck-billed dinosaur, famous because all of the layers of its skin have been preserved and naturally mummified. You can clearly see scale patterns. Dakota is 67 million years old.

Other fossil exhibits include Bison Antiquus, which became extinct 10,000 years ago, Archelon, the 15 foot sea turtle, and Xiphactinus, the scariest fish I've ever seen.

The Native American and pioneer artifacts are spectacular too. My favorite pieces are a warrior's staff he had made to memorialize the horse he lost in the Battle of Little Bighorn, and Sitting Bull's pipe bag.

My favorite army artifacts are a drum from the 1860s used to relay orders from officers to soldiers, a block with soldier's graffiti, and a pocket surgical kit used by the only surgeon to survive the Battle of Little Bighorn.

How to get to the North Dakota Heritage Center & State Museum:

The North Dakota Heritage Center & State Museum is located at 612 E. Boulevard Ave, in Bismarck.

A word about the great blizzard of 1888:

On January 12, 1888, one of the worst blizzards ever recorded sped across the Great Plains states, producing a wall of ice that froze everything in its path. The 1888 blizzard became known as "The School Children's Blizzard," because many of the victims were school children.

The blizzard blew out of Canada and landed down upon North Dakota in the early morning, South Dakota during the morning recess for school children, and Nebraska when school was soon to be dismissed. When the blizzard had passed, animals and people were found frozen to death across the prairie. There were children on their way home from school, found frozen in large drifts of snow, frozen standing up against a tree, or frozen in a haystack. It is estimated that between 250 and 500 people died in the blizzard of 1888.

Menoken Indian Village

T he ***Menoken Indian Village*** was inhabited during the Late Woodland period around 1200 AD. Menoken was once a village of 30 pit houses, inside a defensive palisade and ditches. Its inhabitants lived primarily by bison hunting, with very little farming.

The villagers lived in two types of oval shaped houses, one which was partially underground, and the other on the ground surface.

Excavations at Menoken uncovered artifacts including obsidian. The closest source for obsidian is Yellowstone, a distance of over 500 miles. Tools made of Knife River flint were also found. This highly durable stone came from quarries about 60 miles from Menoken.

Copper artifacts were also found at Menoken. The closest source of copper is in eastern Minnesota. Shell artifacts were also uncovered. The source of these artifacts could have been from the Atlantic Ocean, Gulf of Mexico, or the Caribbean.

How to get to Menoken Indian Village:

The Menoken Indian Village is located near the town of Menoken, about 10 miles east of Bismarck.

A word about war paint:

Native Americans painted their bodies for protection in battle, and to commemorate important events. Common war paint included:

- Painted hands, which indicated the warrior had taken prisoners

- Sticks in the hair, which represented gunshot wounds

- Notched feathers in the hair, which represented cutting an enemy's throat

- Tufted feathers in the hair, which represented taking an enemy's scalp

- Split feathers in the hair, which represented an arrow injury

- Painted feathers in the hair, which represented killing an enemy

Fort Abercrombie

*F*ort Abercrombie was the first permanent fort to be established in the Dakota Territory, on August 28, 1858, by Lieutenant John J. Abercrombie.

The purpose of the fort was to guard wagon trains and steamboats traveling along the Red River. Dakota warriors laid siege to the fort for six weeks during the 1862 Minnesota Indian War. Volunteers defended the fort because the regular military were fighting in the Civil War.

The original guardhouse was used by soldiers on guard duty, who would stand guard for 24 hours. A third of the men would stand guard for 4 hours, and be relieved by the next shift.

Four to five prisoners could be held in the cells within the guard-house.

Fort Abercrombie once had a hospital, brewery, enlisted men's barracks, three corner blockhouses, a guardhouse, and stockade. The fort was abandoned in 1877, and buildings were auctioned to the public.

How to get to Fort Abercrombie:

Fort Abercrombie is located on County Hwy. 22 on the east edge of the town of Abercrombie.

Fort Totten

C onstruction on ***Fort Totten*** began in 1867 and was completed in 1872. The fort is named after Brevet General Joseph Gilbert Totten, who was a chief engineer of the US Army.

The fort was tasked with patrolling the international boundary with British Canada, controlling liquor traffic, and protection of members of the reservation and settlers.

The 7th cavalry was stationed at Fort Totten, including Marcus Reno, Miles Keogh, and his horse Comanche. Comanche was the only horse to survive the Battle of the Little Bighorn. He was returned home to Fort Totten.

Fort Totten was decommissioned in 1890, and was bought by the Bureau of Indian Affairs in 1891. It became an Indian Industrial School from 1891 to 1935, and then a tuberculosis preventorium from 1935 to 1939. After that, Fort Totten became a community school from 1940 to 1959. In 1960, Fort Totten became a State Historic Site.

Today, as you walk around Fort Totten, you can see 16 of the original 39 buildings, including the 1868 Commissary Building, which now houses the gift shop and interpretive center.

The interpretive center contains some interesting artifacts uncovered during archaeological excavations. My favorite is this delicate porcelain dog figurine.

How to get to Fort Totten:

Fort Totten is located at 417 Cavalry Circle, in Fort Totten.

Voices from the past:

"When the commandant is drunk, which is almost every day, he gives himself over to his ridiculous or brutal eccentricities, which, of course, earn him the hatred and scorn of his men." **Colonel de Trobriand commenting on Captain Wainright's drunken behavior, 1867**

Fort Abraham Lincoln

*F*ort *Abraham Lincoln* has a lot of history, but not a lot of structures. There is the reconstructed Officer's Quarters, now known as the Custer House. The original was built in 1872.

Custer lived here from 1873 to when he left to fight the Battle of Little Bighorn in 1876.

The house was closed when I visited, so I took photos from the porch to give an idea of the view of the parade grounds Custer could enjoy when he lived there with his wife, Libby.

How to get to Fort Abraham Lincoln:

Fort Abraham Lincoln is located at 4480 Fort Lincoln Rd, in Mandan.

Ghost story:

Libbie Custer and the officer's wives were gathered at the Custer house when they received news of the massacre of all the soldiers, including their husbands. Visitors and employees at the fort have seen a woman, dressed in black, standing at one of the upstairs windows. The bed in the upstairs bedroom will also occasionally show the imprint of a body weighing it down. Paranormal investigators have also recorded a spirit voice saying "more of the men have been dying" Orser

Profiles in history:

Elizabeth (Libby) Custer was born April 8, 1842, into a life of wealth and privilege. Her father hoped she would marry into a wealthy family. Instead, she fell in love with George Armstrong Custer, a military man of poor means. Libby's father would not allow Custer into the house and forbade her to marry him. Eventually Custer was promoted, and Libby's father gave his consent. She felt it was her duty to inform the other wives of the massacre. She stood by her dead husband's memory, going to great lengths to clear his name. Libby Custer was 90 years old when she died in 1933. She is buried next to her husband in West Point.

George Armstrong Custer was born in Rumley, Ohio, Dec. 5, 1839. A former teacher, he went to the US Military Academy, graduating in 1861. He served in the Civil War, as the youngest Union army general, and had many victories over confederates. He was said to have had horses shot out from under him, and only had one minor injury. Interestingly, Custer was court-martialed for "deserting his post, failure to determine the welfare of some of his men, and using military equipment for personal reasons." He was suspended for one year without pay and reduced to the rank of captain. The story was, he went to defend his wife, who was staying at a nearby camp. Custer died in the battle of Little Bighorn June 25, 1876, following the orders of his commanding General Terry.

Favorite Places to Camp

Van Hook Resort is a beautiful campground on the shores of Lake Sakakawea. They offer a wide range of options. I chose the $15 per night primitive campsite with a world class view. They also have electric sites for $22 per night, and tent sites for $10 per night. For more information or to make a reservation, please visit https://www.vanhookresort.com/

Fort Abraham Lincoln State Park boasts 51 campsites with power, and 15 primitive campsites. It's a lovely area and perfect for exploring the fort. For more information or to make reservations, please visit https://www.parkrec.nd.gov/fort-abraham-lincoln-state-park

There is also plenty of open space in North Dakota for dry camping. Check online at https://www.campendium.com/

Random Thoughts
What History Means to Me

First, let me start by sharing with you my opinion of what history isn't. History is not a collection of random dates, names, and places for you to memorize. History is not a dry and uninteresting class you have to pass to graduate.

I believe history is a tangible thing. You can actually *feel* history in the places you go, and the sights you see. I remember walking up to the Acropolis in Athens. I looked down at the well-worn marble steps and wondered about how many ancient philosophers had climbed these very steps, thousands of years ago.

You don't have to go far away to experience the *feeling* of history. If you are lucky enough to live in an old house, you may experience history in your own surroundings. You might say to yourself, *"If only these walls could talk."*

During my travels across the United States, I *felt* history in many, many places. If you travel across the country like I did, you will *feel* the wonderful history of our beautiful country for yourself, and you will never be the same. You will discover what it means to be an American.

Why I travel, and why you should too:

I decided to travel across the country by car because I wanted to rediscover America. When I first set out to explore the history of our country, I wanted to find out why America is the greatest country on earth, and what it means to be an American.

The politics of these United States can be frightening and polarizing. I prefer to focus on what unites us, not what divides us. What unites us is we all live in a spectacularly beautiful country, with warm, wonderful people.

I began my journey five years ago, starting out in my Honda CRV. I soon realized I loved the lifestyle, so now I travel in a small RV. From my small RV, I look out on a country with a unique and colorful, multicultural tapestry, unlike any other country on earth.

I have a degree in Archaeology, and a passion for all things archaeological. I love history, with a side love of paleontology. It is these three passions that I set my trip agenda around. I set out to discover the archaeological sites, history, and paleontological world of our country.

As I travel and write my books, I get asked all the time, especially by women, "What is it like to travel by yourself? Aren't you scared?" The truth is, I believe everyone should do what I did. It's a wonderful way to discover our country, and to rediscover yourself. The truth is, I'm scared not to travel. Traveling allows you to get to know yourself, in ways not possible when sitting on the couch watching TV.

We tend to spend a lot of our lives tuning out the world and our place within it. When you travel, you are quite literally forced to deal with your own thoughts, emotions, and feelings. You can discover yourself while traveling. You can come to understand what makes you who you are, and how you can perhaps become a better person. Above all, traveling gives you mental clarity to figure out how to live with intent. It's a way to guide your life, not just wait for things to happen.

Travel Tips & Stuff

What You Need to Know

How to get started:

P lanning your trip should be one of the most exciting things about it. You want to be spontaneous, but it is also very wise to plan your route, so you can take full advantage of all the time and miles you will invest.

- First, decide your passions. If you love airplanes, trains, or old vehicles, plan your trip around that. If you love gardens or architecture, seek that out as the focus of your trip.

- Next, read and research areas of the country that will let you enjoy what you are interested in.

- Make a list by state and city or town, of what you want to see.

- Take your handy road atlas and locate the areas on the pages.

- Make a tentative route plan, so you have an idea of where you are going.

Travel tip: Avoid trying to plan your trip down to a schedule of days, hours, or minutes. On a road trip, it will be virtually impossible to know where you will be on any given day. If you adhere to a schedule, you are more likely to stress out, and less likely to actually enjoy yourself, which is the whole point.

What you need:

You need to bring along a sense of adventure and a curious mind. You need to ditch the idea of always being on a schedule, and live a little more spontaneously to thoroughly enjoy yourself. Things will happen as you travel, both good things and bad things, and you need to prepare your mind and your soul for day-to-day changes.

So much of our lives are planned out. Between growing up, going to school, finding a career, marriage, kids, or whatever, people have lost much of the ability to be spontaneous. But you must take spontaneity on the trip with you, because you may make detours along the way to see something really spectacular.

So, for the practical stuff you need:

A great vehicle-I am now five years into the trip and have swapped out my Honda CRV for a small RV, just under 20 feet. I go small because I see humongous RVs on the road, towing a car behind, and all I can think of is, they can't go just anywhere. They are too big. Bad gas mileage, cumbersome to drive, slow, and not agile like my small RV. So, I encourage you, if you want to go car or RV camping and be able to go on remote dirt roads, get an agile vehicle, and small RVs are great.

Travel tip: Don't be afraid to do some modifications to your vehicle. I have made many alterations to my RV, including changing the plumbing, which used to be a mere 4 inches off of the ground, so I would break it all the time. It's now encased in my outside storage compartment. I am also a minimalist, so I have jettisoned anything I won't use or don't love. Don't be afraid to get rid of unnecessary stuff.

An awesome camera that you know inside and out. I use a Nikon and it takes wonderful pictures. Don't skimp on a camera, and don't think a cellphone camera is all you need, because you want the best for your beautiful photos.

Window shades-the best ones are magnetic so you just place them against your windows and they cling to them, obscuring the view inside your car. I also have magnetic window screens, so I can leave my windows down with no bugs!

Battery operated fans and lights-these are important, so you don't have to rely on your house batteries for light and cooling options.

Portable air compressor-this little gem plugs into your cigarette lighter and will inflate your tires if you have a flat. Make sure the air compressor can reach to all of your tires, including your rear tires.

Portable battery charger and power bank-mine comes with battery cables and the power bank, yet once inside the case, it is small enough to put in your glove compartment. This little item, unfortunately, I have had to use, and it saved me.

Portable generator-I have two gas powered generators on the back of my RV, which are hooked together with a coupling unit. I have an interior generator, but after much expense and multiple repairs, it still doesn't work. Now I have generators which will run everything, including AC, and I can maintain them myself.

All season clothing-you never know what different states will bring for weather, so take hot weather and cold weather clothes, and a fair amount of shoes appropriate for hiking, or walking, sandals, and slippers, which are nice at night. Also take along a pair of cheap rubber flip-flops to wear in the public showers you might go into.

Your own pillows-I like my own pillows, so I don't wake up with neck cramps, especially after sleeping in the car.

Sleeping bag and cozy blankets-you want to stay warm and layering is everything.

Warm hat, warm socks, and fuzzy jammies to keep you warm for cold nights sleeping in the car.

A great road atlas, and great guidebooks-get one that's easy to read, with great pictures. For a road atlas, just get one that is easy to read.

A word about photography:

Along with a great camera, you need to have a great eye. This is easier than it sounds once you have worked with your camera and are comfortable taking pictures with it. I am not a professional photographer, but I like my pictures and other people do too.

These are my tips for taking great pictures:

- Experiment with taking both horizontal and vertical shots.

- Don't always put the subject of the photo in the middle of the photograph.

- This one is important: pay attention to the foreground, and if possible, have something, a plant or whatever, in the foreground to help give the photo dimension and depth.

- This one is important too: turn around often to see the view you just came from. I do this quite often and some of my best pictures have resulted from when I turned around and took the shot.

You can also take a mental photo. Place an image in your mind that you can call upon later. Use all of your senses to see, hear, smell, and maybe even to taste, what is around you. You have the means to fully experience your surroundings, and that is very important to a traveler. When you take a mental photo, be sure to jot down quick little details about what you saw, heard, smelled, or tasted, so you can jog your memory later.

And last, but not least...don't be posing in front of everything, everywhere, to show that you actually went somewhere. Most people want to see themselves in your photo and be mentally transported there, but they can't if you are there already.⫻

To camp or not to camp:

Car or RV camping is great. I prefer it to sleeping on the cold, hard ground in a tent. I can lock the doors, put my window shades up and be cozy for the night.

Some people camp in a Walmart parking lot and feel safe. I do not. I believe that if you are in a busy area, you are more likely to be confronted by a nut job who may bother you. Nothing against Walmart, and many Walmart stores don't allow overnight parking. I don't go for rest areas either because they have a track record of incidents happening to people in rest areas, especially women travelers.

I have come to love casino parking lots. I enjoy gambling, so for a little money, many casinos will provide overnight stays if you gamble a little inside the casino. I also do a lot of boondocking, because it's free, and I believe you are safer parked out in the middle of nowhere in the dark.

I also enjoy camping in state or national campgrounds, wildlife sanctuaries, and fairgrounds.

A word about safety:

When you are a woman traveling alone, it's critical to keep a low profile. Don't tell people you are traveling alone, where you are staying, or any other personal information.

I don't go to bars or get drunk. I'm not preaching but you are on your own, in a city or town you've never been to, and you don't know anyone, so it's not the time to lose control of what you are doing. When you are in control, you are better able to decide which people you want to get to know better.

Travel tip: If you feel vulnerable traveling alone, that's OK. Vulnerability is part of passion, and traveling is a passionate thing to do. You can put one of those family stickers on your vehicle to indicate to others that you are not traveling alone, which can help you feel more secure.

Maintain your connections:

When you are traveling alone, there is a definite sense of disconnection. It feels almost like you are the only one in the world, traveling through space and time. That's why it's critical to keep your connections to loved ones active.

Be on Facebook while you are traveling. You may not have internet a lot of the time, or the internet will be poor. Consider paying to have your phone be a hotspot. It's a little bit of money per month, but it's worth it and has saved me from being without internet. I love the convenience of it, and you will too.

Plan your journey around visiting family members or friends you haven't seen for a long time, or people that are good friends. When you see people you know, it will ground you, so you can continue traveling.

Check in by phone with loved ones. They worry about you, and it's good for both of you to stay connected no matter where you are.

Consider traveling with a pet. I now travel with my 12 year-old sheltie Rosie, after losing my beloved sheltie, Sadie. Rosie is a wonderful companion. She is also an excellent watchdog, and barks her head off at other dogs and people.

Travel tip: One of the easiest and best ways I stay connected while traveling is to offer to take a photo for someone I don't know. Many couples, families, or singles would love to have more pictures of themselves traveling. It's an easy and quick way to have a connection with a fellow traveler, and it's good manners too.

Practical matters:

You need to have an address to send your mail to. Keep in touch with whomever is nice enough to do this for you.

You will also need to come back occasionally to register your car, vote, go to doctor visits, and take care of any other business. You can't leave it all behind, as tempting as that may be.

Bad things that happened:

I have had a few problems, mostly associated with my RV. I bought an older model, vintage 1999, and I have had to do a few repairs.

My worst experience came when I took my rig in to a shop in Spokane, Washington (who shall remain nameless.) All I needed was an oil change. I got the oil change and was about an hour south of town on a Friday at 4:30, when my engine blew.

I was in the middle of the eastern Washington prairie, many miles from the nearest town. All I could do was watch my oil drain out onto the Interstate. I can't help but think it was associated with my oil change, but I couldn't prove it. The moral of this story is: DON'T LET JUST ANYONE WORK ON YOUR VEHICLE.

Good things that happened:

I have met many great people on my travels, from all walks of life. I have also learned not to judge people. I have met numerous homeless people who are often just wanting a kind word, and not to be treated like dirt.

People have mistaken me for a homeless person, and I too, have been treated like dirt. When I can, I try to help people and be kind to them. Most of the time, they smile and reciprocate. You will always meet people who are unkind, but they are just as likely to be driving a huge expensive rig, or to be homeless.

We are all Americans, and we are all part of the human race. When you meet people across the country, you realize just how important it is to get to know your fellow citizens, and learn more about how they view the world and our country.

I have to give a special shout-out to the many dedicated people, often volunteers, who staff our state and national parks and monuments. They work tirelessly to ensure the health of our natural resources, and help travelers enjoy their visit. The same is true of the many people who staff the museums in small towns and large cities. They enjoy history, like I do, and it shows in their smiles.

Along with wonderful people, I have seen an America that is spectacularly beautiful, with open prairies, majestic mountains, and crystal clear rivers. I have seen a small fraction of the history of our country. I have seen the memorials to the brave people who shaped our country. I have fallen in love with America in a way that was not possible sitting in my living room. People ask me, "would I do it again?" The answer comes easily, "Yes, in a heartbeat."

Bibliography and Further Reading

Aasen, Lawrence O. *North Dakota Postcards*, 1900-1930. Arcadia Pub., 2000.

California Trail, National Park Service.

Donovan, Jim. *A Terrible Glory: Custer and the Little Bighorn-the Last Great Battle of the American West*. Back Bay Books, 2009.

Enss, Chris. *Tales behind the Tombstones*. Morris Pub., 2007.

Finch, etc. al.., Jackie. *Eyewitness Travel USA*. DK Publishing, 2017.

Glassman, Steve. *It Happened on the Santa Fe Trail*. Twodot, 2008.

Hill, William E. *The Oregon Trail, Yesterday and Today: a Brief History and Pictorial Journey along the Wagon Tracks of Pioneers*. Caxton Press, 2014.

Jones, Landon Y. *The Essential Lewis and Clark*. Harper Collins Publishers, 2000.

Knife River Indian Villages, National Park Service, 2015.

Laskin, David, *The Children's Blizzard*, Harper Collins, 2004.

Lewis and Clark National and State Historical Parks, National Park Service.

Orser, Lori, Spooky Creepy North Dakota, Schiffer Publishing, 2010.

Peck, David J. *Or Perish in the Attempt: The Hardship and Medicine of the Lewis and Clark Expedition*. The History Press, 2002.

Wagner, Tricia Martineau. *It Happened on the Oregon Trail: Remarkable Events That Shaped History*. GPP, 2014.

Welcome to Fort Abercrombie State Historic Site, State Historical Society of North Dakota.

Welcome to Fort Buford State Historic Site, State Historical Society of North Dakota.

Welcome to Fort Clark State Historic Site, State Historical Society of North Dakota.

Welcome to Fort Dilts State Historic Site, State Historical Society of North Dakota.

Welcome to Kildeer Mountain Battlefield, State Historical Society of North Dakota.

Welcome to Fort Mandan State Historic Site, State Historical Society of North Dakota.

Welcome to Fort Totten State Historic Site, State Historical Society of North Dakota.

Index

Referenced by Sections

D

F

G

H

I

J

K

L

Lake Sakakawea-see Favorite Places to Camp

Lakota Sioux-see Killdeer Mountain Battlefield

L'Amour, Louis-see Famous Citizens of North Dakota

Late Woodland period-see Menoken Indian Village

Lee, Peggy-see Famous Citizens of North Dakota

Lemhi Shoshone-see Fort Mandan

Lewis & Clark Expedition-see Knife River Indian Villages, Fort Mandan,

Lewis, Meriwether-see Fort Mandan, Lewis & Clark Interpretive Center

M

Mandan--see Knife River Indian Villages, Fort Clark

Maximillian, Prince of Wied-see Lewis & Clark Interpretive Center

Medicine Bear-see Killdeer Mountain Battlefield

Minnesota Indian War-see Fort Abercrombie

N

Nakota Sioux-see Killdeer Mountain Battlefield

About the Author

Julie Bettendorf is a world traveler with a degree in archaeology and a background in history. She has traveled extensively throughout Egypt, Central America, South America, Europe, and the United Kingdom, visiting archaeological and historical sites all along the way.

Currently, Julie is traveling around the US visiting ghost towns, ancient rock art sites, and archaeological wonders as part of research for her ongoing historical travel series entitled ***Wandering Woman***. Wandering Woman is a set of state-by-state guides, full of photographs, historical anecdotes, and unique tips to help other women travel and explore solo across the US by car or RV. Julie enjoys writing freelance blogs, traveling frequently with her two adult children, and hiking outdoors with her faithful dog companion Rosie.

Also By Julie Bettendorf

Wandering Woman: North Dakota is the most recent book in the ***Wandering Woman Travel Series***. The first books on ***Montana***, ***Utah, Colorado, Oregon, Washington, Idaho, Northern California, Southern California, Arizona, New Mexico, Nevada, Wyoming, Kansas, Nebraska, and South Dakota,*** are available in ebook and paperback.

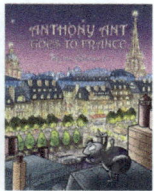

Julie has published two children's books in an ongoing, beautifully illustrated travel series entitled ***Anthony Ant Goes to France*** and ***Anthony Ant Goes to Egypt***.

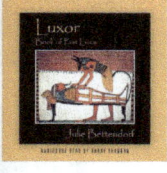

She has also published a work of historical fiction entitled ***Luxor: Book of Past Lives*** which has recently been released as an audiobook, read by renowned narrator Barry Shannon.